A Mo Adventure

by Gretchen Carter

Illustrated by Pat Paris

Editorial Offices: Glenview, Illinois • Parsippany, New Jersey • New York, New York
Sales Offices: Needham, Massachusetts • Duluth, Georgia • Glenview, Illinois
Coppell, Texas • Sacramento, California • Mesa, Arizona

backpack

Mt. Washington is the tallest mountain in New England.

Linda was excited. Today she would hike Mount Washington. Her Girl Scout leaders, Mrs. Martínez and Mrs. Chang, loved to hike. They knew a lot about hiking and mountain safety.

Mount Washington is in New Hampshire. It is the tallest mountain in New England. It is almost 6,300 feet high.

Sometimes Mount Washington has some of the worst weather in the world. The highest wind speed ever was measured there. The wind blew at 231 miles per hour during a storm in 1934.

New Hampshire: a state in New England

The girls camped near the mountain. They woke up early and ate breakfast. It was a sunny July day.

"Look at this blade of grass," Inez said. "Why is it wet?"

"That water is morning dew," Linda said.

The group got ready. They hoped to see some snow. The snow would be in a shady, cool spot.

Mount Washington can get twenty-six feet of snow in a year! So much snow can take a long time to melt.

Mrs. Martínez led the way. There were seven girls and two adults. Mrs. Chang made sure everyone hiked safely.

Everyone had a full backpack. The hikers needed lots of water, snacks, and lunch. They had extra clothes too. Everyone needed a jacket, a raincoat, hat, and mittens. Even in summer, mountain weather can be cold.

"As we climb higher," Mrs. Chang said, "the weather will get colder."

The girls hiked higher and higher. They swatted bugs. They drank bottles of water.

"I'm tired," Inez said.

After a rest and a snack, Linda and Inez sang songs. Inez felt better.

They saw chipmunks. A hawk flew high in the sky.

"Hiking is hard work," Linda said, "but I love it!"

---

swatted: hit away

The girls ate lunch beside a ranger station. A ranger talked to them about Mount Washington.

"You are lucky," the ranger said. "The weather is perfect today. Storms can be so bad on this mountain. Bad weather can make hiking dangerous."

"Will we see snow?" Linda asked.

"Yes," the ranger said. "There is plenty of snow left on parts of the mountain."

---

ranger station: an office for rangers
ranger: a worker who guards or cares for park land

The group hiked higher up Mount Washington. Linda found the snow first.

"I can't believe there is snow in July," Linda shouted. "My brother won't believe me!"

The girls put on their jackets, gloves, and hats, and they played in the snow. They felt chilly now. The wind blew. They were happy to have warm clothes.

After fun, rest, and another snack, Mrs. Martínez called the girls. "We have to hike back now," she said.

---

chilly: cold

"Can we come again next summer?" Inéz asked.

"Please!" Linda said. "Next year I want to hike to the top!"

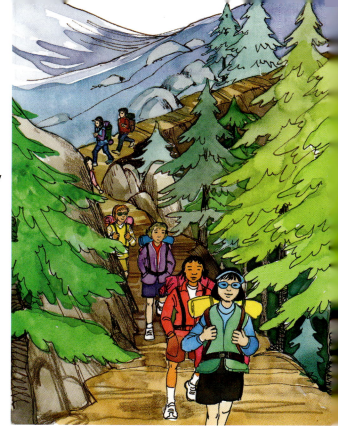

Rules for Safe Hikes

- Stay with your group. Stay on the trail.
- Bring plenty of food and water.
- Bring the right clothes.
- Be careful of bad weather.
- Bring a first aid kit.
- Wear a whistle. Blow it if you get lost.
- Do not keep hiking if you are lost. Stay in one safe place. Wait for help. If someone has a wireless phone, call for help.